Anonymous

Woman's Wisdom

A collection of choice recipes

Anonymous

Woman's Wisdom
A collection of choice recipes

ISBN/EAN: 9783337426699

Printed in Europe, USA, Canada, Australia, Japan

Cover: Foto ©Lupo / pixelio.de

More available books at **www.hansebooks.com**

Woman's Wisdom,

A

Collection of

Choice Recipes.

—

Published by

Ladies' Society

of the

First Presbyterian Church,

Owensboro, Kentucky.

O. T. Kendall,
1890.
Owensboro, Ky.

PRESBYTERIAN CHURCH
OWENSBORO, KY

OTIS DOCKSTADER ARCHITECT,
ELMIRA, NY

PREFACE.

IT has not been the intention of the compilers of this book to originate anything new in the way of culinary lore, so much as to gather into one volume a collection of practical recipes as used by experienced cooks. These have all been thoroughly tested by those who know them to be perfectly reliable. In some cases certain articles are recommended in the preparation of the recipes. They are in every respect just what they are represented,—goods of superior excellence, manufactured in a careful and wholesome manner.

It is the hope of those interested in the publication of this book, that it may prove a safe and trusted guide to housekeepers, in supplying their tables with those delicacies wheih render them attractive and inviting. We hope, also, by the sale of the book, to assist in furnishing our new Church; to which cause we devote the proceeds of our efforts.

THE COMPILERS.

Measures and Weights.

Two cupfuls of butter................................... 1 pound
One quart of flour.................................... 1   "
Two cupfuls of sugar, granulated...................... 1   "
Two heaping cupfuls of sugar, powdered................ 1   "
One pint of liquid.................................... 1   "
One pint of finely chopped meat....................... 1   "

Rule for Cooking Vegetables.

Asparagus 30   60 minutes.
Beets....................................... 1   3 hours.
Cabbage..................................... 1   2 hours.
Carrots..................................... 1   2 hours.
Green Corn.................................. 30   60 minutes.
Onions...................................... 2   3 hours.
Parsnips .... 1 hour.
Peas .... 1 hour.
Potatoes, baked .... 45 minutes.
Potatoes, boiled............................ 30   40 minutes.
Shell beans .... 1 - 2 hours.
String beans................................ 2 hours.
Spinach..................................... 20   30 minutes.
Squash, baked............................... 1 hour.
Squash, boiled.............................. 30 minutes.
Tomatoes .... 30 minutes.
Turnips..................................... 1 hour.

Rule for Canning Fruits.

Apples, sour ....   Boil 10 minutes.   6 oz. sugar per lb.
Pears.......................   Boil 8 minutes.   6   "   "
Cherries....................   Boil 5 minutes.   8   "   "   "
Raspberries ....   Boil 6 minutes.   4   "   "
Blackberries ....   Boil 6 minutes.   6   "   "   "
Plums ....   Boil 10 minutes.   6   "   "   "
Strawberries ....   Boil 8 minutes.   8   "   "   "
Peaches.....................   Boil 10 minutes.   4   "   "   "
Currants....................   Boil 6 minutes.   8   "   "   "
Grapes......................   Boil 10 minutes.   8   "   "   "
Pineapple...................   Boil 10 minutes.   6   "   "   "
Tomatoes....................   Boil 20 minutes.

SOUPS.

BEEF SOUP.

Take a five-cent soup bone; put on early in the morning. Let it simmer until about ten o'clock, then add a pint of butter-beans, corn and potatoes, a quart of tomatoes, two or three carrots, and turnips, in fact any kind of vegetables. Let it boil until dinner-time, then strain, and if not thick enough, thicken with a tablespoonful of flour in cold water—add salt, pepper, a pinch of ginger, allspice, cloves, mace. Let it boil up and serve.　　　　　　　　　　　　Mrs. B. W. G.

BEEF SOUP.

A twenty-cent soup bone, simmer in a large kettle of water six or eight hours. Remove the meat, strain the liquor. Set away until next morning. Remove the fat which has risen. At ten o'clock put stock over to boil; two large onions, sliced; add three carrots, cut in dice; six potatoes; whole peppercorns. Just before serving add two tablespoonfuls tomato catsup or half can tomatoes strained; one tablespoonful of flour creamed with two of butter.　　　　　Mrs. L. B. T.

BOUILLON.

Made same as above, omitting all vegetables. Just before taking up add a tablespoonful of caromel to give an amber color. Season only with pepper and salt.

　　　　　　　　　　　　　　　　Mrs. L. B. T.

CALF'S-HEAD SOUP.

After the head is thoroughly cleansed boil it in a

large pot of water until the bones can be taken out. Brown two tablespoonfuls of flour in another pot, and strain the liquor from the head on it. Put it on to boil with two large onions, a few cloves, a small cupful of powdered allspice, pepper and salt combined. In about an hour add the head cut up into small pieces. Pick out the brains and beat them up with flour, butter and chopped parsley to thicken the soup. Boil one hour after the head is put in, add force meat balls and two hard boiled eggs chopped fine. For the force meat, chop cold lean ham, or cold veal, mix with a raw egg. Make into balls and fry in butter.　　　　　Mrs. M. A. T.

CHICKEN SOUP.

The water in which chicken has been boiled will make excellent soup, by adding a few tablespoonsful of rice, cooked; a little thickening, salt and pepper—also, a few sprigs of parsley or celery, chopped fine. A little celery seed may be used instead.　　　　Mrs. S. C. W.

CORN AND TOMATO SOUP.

Save the water in which a leg of mutton has been boiled. When cold remove the fat. The next day put the liquor over, with eight large tomatoes cut in pieces, and twelve ears of corn, use the corn cut from cob, also the cobs, to give it a sweet flavor. Boil slowly for four hours. Season with salt and pepper, strain through a colander and serve.　　　　　Mrs. S. T. L.

BRUNSWICK STEW.

Two chickens or squirrels, one quart of tomatoes, peeled and sliced; one pint butter-beans; six potatoes, parboiled and sliced; six ears green corn, cut from the

cob ; one-half pound butter, one-half pound fat, salt
pork ; one-half teaspoon cayenne pepper, one tablespoon salt, two tablespoons sugar, one onion, sliced fine;
one gallon water. Boil slowly two hours and a half.
Ten minutes before taking from fire, add butter rolled in
flour, in small lumps. Mrs. A. S. B.

POTATO SOUP.

Half a dozen large potatoes sliced thin, one quart of
water. Cook until tender Add a pint of rich sweet
milk, thicken with flour or cornstarch ; add butter size
of an egg, a little rice or macaroni may be used, but it
is not necessary. This soup is good for invalids.

Mrs. L. G. W.

GREEN PEA SOUP.

Take a chicken, after it has been cut up put in a
quart and a half of water, a little parsley, one onion cut
up, pepper and salt, two spoons of butter, one quart of
peas after being shelled. When the peas have been
boiled until they can be mashed, take them out, mash
and strain through a colander, and put back in the soup.
Let them boil a short time, then add butter mixed with
a little flour. Just before taking off stir in a teacup of
cream. Any kind of fresh meats will answer.

Mrs. B. W. G.

TOMATO SOUP.

Six large tomatoes and one quart of boiling water.
Boil until thoroughly tender then strain through a seive.
Add to the liquor one-half teaspoon of soda ; salt, pepper and butter to taste. Pour over a few rolled crackers. Mrs. M. F. V. R.

BEAN SOUP.

Three pints of beans, half gallon of water. Boil one hour, then add a small piece of bacon ; season to taste with pepper, and boil another hour. It will likely be thick enough, and is good warmed over, with a little water, for next day.　　　　　Mrs. L. G. W.

CANNED CORN SOUP.

One can of corn, drained and chopped fine, one quart of boiling water, three tablespoonfuls of butter, rolled in one tablespoonful of flour, two eggs, one tablespoonful of sugar ; salt and pepper. Boil one minute and stir in flour and butter. Have one quart of scalding hot milk and add it slowly to the beaten eggs. When the butter is thoroughly melted, stir eggs and milk into the soup ; boil one minute and pour out.　　　　　Mrs. L. G. P.

CREAM OF CELERY SOUP.

A pint of milk, a tablespoonful of flour and one of butter, a head of celery, a large slice of onion and a small piece of mace. Boil celery in a pint of water, from thirty to forty minutes ; boil mace, onion and milk together, mix flour with two tablespoons of cold milk and add to boiling milk, cook ten minutes. Mash celery in the water in which it has been boiled, and stir with boiling milk ; add butter, and season with salt and pepper to taste, strain and serve immediately. The flavor is improved by adding a cupful of whipped cream when the soup is in the tureen.　　　　　Mrs. B. W. G.

MOCK BISQUE SOUP.

A quart can of tomatoes, three quarts of milk, a large tablespoonful of flour, butter the size of an egg, pepper and salt to taste ; a scant teaspoon of soda. Put the tomatoes on to stew, and the milk in a double kettle to boil, reserving, however, half a cupful to mix with flour. Mix the flour smoothly with the cold milk, stir into the boiling milk and cook ten minutes. To the tomatoes add the soda, stir well and rub through a strainer that is fine enough to keep back the seeds ; add butter, salt and pepper to the milk, and then the tomatoes ; serve immediately. If half the rule is made, stir the tomatoes well in the can before dividing, as the liquor portion is more acid.　　　　　　　　　　　　Mrs. B. W. G.

CROUTONS.

Small pieces of bread, cut in dice and fried brown, to be used in soup.

CAROMEL FOR SOUP.

Put a teacup of sugar in a small fry pan, and set over the fire ; stir continually until it is a bright brown color and sends forth a burning smell ; add half a pint of vinegar, boil, and when cool, bottle. Add to soups at discretion.　　　　　　　　　　　Mrs. L. B. T.

FISH AND OYSTERS.

Ohio River fish is improved by being put on ice over night.

BOILED CAT FISH.

The fish should weigh from six to ten pounds. Roll securely in a cloth, (with head on) cover with water. Boil from one and a half to two hours, according to size of fish. When done unpin the cloth and roll on fish dish whole, cover with "egg gravy." Garnish dish with nasturtium, flowers and leaves, or parsley. Mrs. S. C. W.

EGG GRAVY.

Take a pint of "chicken-water"; add three or four hard boiled eggs, well chopped; a lump of butter about the size of a walnut, rolled in flour; salt and pepper to suit taste; boil in a sauce-pan to thicken.

This receipt may be used for boiled fish, substituting plain water; also add a teaspoon of mixed or flour of mustard. Mrs. S. C. W.

FRIED FISH.

Get a fish about eight inches long, leave as whole as possible in dressing. Have ready a frying pan of hot lard; salt, dredge in meal and fry to a beautiful brown. Take up the instant it is done. Mrs. N. M. A.

BAKED FISH.

Use a white fish or salmon, weighing three or four pounds. Prepare a rich stuffing of bread-crumbs. Fill the fish and tie or sew firmly. Lay thin slices of bacon over it, place in a pan containing a little water, baste frequently. Bake two hours. Mrs. L. B. T.

TURBOT.

Five pounds of white fish, boil and cool. For dressing, take one quart of milk, one-quarter pound of flour. Wet with a little milk; one-quarter pound of butter, two eggs, two small onions, one-half bunch of thyme, one-half bunch of parsley, pepper and salt. Boil together until it thickens. Put in the baking dish a layer of fish, then a layer of dressing, a layer of bread crumbs. Grate cheese over the top, and bake half an hour.

Mrs. A. G. C.

CODFISH OMELETTE.

Pick up one cup of salt codfish, soak over night in just enough water to cover. Press dry and chop very fine. Put in three gills of milk, and let come to a boil. Stir one tablespoon of flour in butter half as large as an egg. Stir in thoroughly, then add three eggs well beaten, separately. Turn into a buttered dish, set in a hot oven until it rises and browns over the top.   Mrs. L. B. T.

CLAM SOUP.

Thirty small clams, scrubbed well with a brush and rinsed clean. Place in the oven in a dripping pan; as soon as they open remove the clams carefully, saving the liquor. Chop the clams fine, mix with the liquor, boil twenty minutes. Add a quart of milk, a dozen peppercorns, a dash of onion, a tablespoon of flour creamed with a tablespoon of butter. Boil up and serve.

Mrs. L. B. T.

OYSTER SOUP.

Wash a quart of oysters, then place in a kettle with a little cold water to plump. When hot skim out and set in a warm place, covered to keep hot. Add a quart of boiling water, pepper and salt, and half a cup of butter. When boiling add a quart of hot milk. When this comes to a boil add the oysters. Boil up once then pour over a bowl of broken crackers in a tureen. Serve hot.

Mrs. S. T. L.

FRIED OYSTERS.

Wash oysters, dry them in a cloth, dip in beaten egg then in cracker crumbs salted. If preferred dip twice Then cook in boiling hot lard, take up, place on brown paper to absorb the grease, and serve at once.

Mrs. N. M. A.

PANNED OYSTERS.

Wash a quart of oysters. Toss into a spider a large cup butter, a teaspoonful of salt, a dash of pepper. When hot add the oysters. Cook two minutes then serve on dry toast. Mrs. S. T. L.

OYSTER PATES.

Make a rich puff paste and cut into round cakes, those intended for the bottom crust less than ⅛ inch thick, for the upper a little thicker. With a smaller cutter remove a round of paste from the middle of the latter, leaving a neat ring. Lay this carefully upon the bottom crust; place a second ring upon this, that the cavity may be deep enough to hold the oysters; lay the pieces you have extracted also in the pan with the rest, and bake in a *quick* oven. When done wash over with beaten egg and set in the oven to glaze. Fill the cavity with the mixture prepared as below, fit on the top and serve.

Mixture: One qt. of oysters, one cup of cream, one heaping tablespoonful of butter, one half cup of liquor from the oysters, two tablespoonfuls of corn starch, wet with a little milk; salt and pepper to taste. Boil all except the oysters a few minutes until it thickens, then pour in the ' oysters, boil one minute and fill the cavity in the paste shells. These shells can be bought in most cities, and then the dish is easily prepared.

OYSTER PIE.

Make a nice' puff paste, fill a pudding-dish with slices of bread, cover this with the puff paste. When baked take off the crust and remove the bread; fill with creamed oysters. Send to the table very hot.

CREAMED OYSTERS.

Fifty large oysters, one quart sweet cream, butter, pepper and salt to taste. Put the cream and oysters in separate kettles to heat, let them come to a boil; when sufficiently cooked, skim them, take out oysters and put in a bowl to keep warm; put cream and oyster-liquor together, season to taste and thicken with powdered crackers; when thick as cream add oysters.

MRS. L. B. T.

SALMON CROUQUETTES.

Half can of salmon, remove skin and bones, pour off the liquor and mash very fine. Take half as much mashed potato as salmon, break into it two eggs, one tablespoon Worcestershire Sauce, salt and cayenne pepper to taste. Beat all thoroughly, roll into shape, dip in egg and bread crumbs, and fry in lard. MRS. B. W. G.

MEATS.

"OLD-FASHIONED" STEAK.

Beat the steak until tender, cut in small pieces and drop in cool water. Roll in flour, season with salt and pepper and fry in hot lard like chicken.

MRS. L. G. W.

PANNED STEAK.

Beat the steak, have a skillet very hot and perfectly dry. Put in the steak and as soon as it is seared on one side turn over. Season the seared side with but-

ter, salt and pepper. Turn and season again. The
oftener it is turned and seasoned the better.

Mrs. L. G. W.

FRENCH HASH.

Use ⅓ potatos, ⅔ meat. Chop cold meat and po-
toes fine, mix with one beaten egg, salt and pepper, butter size of an egg, juice of a lemon and enough cream
or rich milk to moisten sufficiently to roll into form.
Make a roll of the mixture, bake on a biscuit pan for
half an hour. Serve with drawn butter poured around
the roll. Mrs. S. T. L.

BREAKFAST OR TEA DISH.

An excellent dish for breakfast or tea can be made
with the cold veal left from dinner. Melt two teaspoon-
fuls of butter in the frying-pan, add one teaspoonful of
flour and stir till smooth ; then add one cupful of water,
or stock if you have it, and season with and salt and
pepper. When it boils add one quart of coarsely chopped cold veal. Let this heat thoroughly ; then dish it
up on slices of nicely browned toast. A dropped egg
put on the middle of each slice of toast and veal is liked
by some. Serve all as hot as possible. Mrs. A. S. B.

BEEF AU GRATIN.

Take cold roast or boiled beef, cut in small pieces ;
butter a dish, sprinkle with bread crumbs, then meat ;
season with salt and pepper, then another of bread ; and
so on, till the dish is full. Pour over half a cup of water
or beef stock, and bake half an hour. Mrs. S. T. L.

BEEF CAKE.

Three pounds beef, cut fine ; 2 eggs, 1 cup milk, 3

slices bread, chopped ; 1 teaspoon pepper, 1 saltspoon salt, 1 tablespoon butter. Bake 1½ hours.

Mrs. L. B. T.

TONGUE.

After boiling as usual until tender, cut in small pieces and brown with flour and butter. Add some stock, season highly, let boil a few minutes and serve hot.

Mrs. H. R.

VEAL LOAF.

Three pounds veal, 1 pound salt pork, 1 dining-plate bread crumbs, 1 nutmeg, 1 tablespoon pepper. Chop the meat ; mix eggs with the crumbs, add to the meat and bake one hour.

Mrs. L. B. T.

TO PREPARE SWEET-BREADS.

Carefully pull off all tough skin. Place in a dish of cold water for 10 minutes. Always boil them 20 minutes, no matter what the mode of cooking is to be.

BROILED SWEETBREADS.

Split the boiled sweet-bread, sprinkle with flour, season with salt, pepper and plenty of butter. Broil ten minutes over a quick fire, turning constantly. Serve with cream sauce.

Mrs. B. W. G.

BREADED SWEET-BREADS.

After being boiled, season with salt and pepper. Dip in beaten egg and cracker crumbs. Fry a light brown, in hot lard, and serve with tomato sauce.

RAGOUT OF MUTTON.

Three pounds of any of the cheap parts of mutton,

6 tablespoons butter, 3 of flour, a large onion, a large white turnip, cut into small tubes, salt and pepper, a quart of water, a bouquet of sweet herbs. Cut the meat in small slices. Put 3 tablespoonfuls of butter and 3 of flour into a stew-pan; when smooth and hot, add the meat. Cook until a rich brown, then add water and set where it will simmer. Put 3 tablespoons of butter in a frying-pan, when hot add onion and turnip, with a teaspoon of flour. Stir constantly until a golden brown, then drain and put with the meat. Simmer 1½ hours, garnish with rice, macaroni or mashed potatoes. Serve hot. Small cubes of potato can be added half an hour before serving. Mrs. B. W. G.

SAUCE FOR MUTTON.

Skim ½ pint of water in which mutton has been boiled. Beat 2 eggs, stir them in the gravy with a tablespoon of flour. Let it stay on the fire until thick. Half a cup of butter must also be used. Mrs. DR. C. H. T.

MINT SUACE.

One cup of minced spearmint, one-half cup of vinegar, ½ cup of hot water, one tablespoon of sugar. Heat to the boiling point. Mrs. S. T. L.

TO BAKE A HAM.

For a 15-pound ham boil two hours; skim and trim the edges, stick cloves all over the fat, half an inch apart; sprinkle a small quantity of ground cinnamon, mace, and allspice over it, then a thick layer of fine bread crumbs; bake 2½ hours in a very slow oven, basting every 15 minutes with the following mixture: 2 teacups molasses, 1 teacup sharp vinegar, 1 teacup water. The ham is improved by boiling one day and baking the second day. Mrs. L. B. T.

VEGETABLES.

BOILED POTATOES.

Water should be boiling when potatoes are put in.
When soft, pour off water, letting them stand on the
stove a few minutes to dry. Then mash well, adding
cream, butter and salt. Beat hard. If cream sauce is
to be used, take a pint of fresh milk; when it comes to
a boil, stir in flour until as thick as desired. Season
with salt and pepper.　　　　　　Mrs. S. C. W.

Baked potatoes must be eaten as soon as they are
done. When they are taken from the oven they should
be put into a napkin or towel and the skin broken, so
as to allow the steam to escape; this will keep the potatoes mealy. If it cools without breaking the skin it
will be watery and have an acid taste, which is caused
by the retaining of a kind of juice which lies next the
skin.　　　　　　Mrs. S. C. S.

LYONNAISE POTATOES.

One qt. cold, chopped potatoes, 2 tablespoon chopped
onion, salt and pepper. Fry the onions until a light
brown in 2 tablespoons butter. Add the potato and seasoning, also 3 tablespoons more butter and stir with a
fork five minutes.　　　　　　Mrs. S. T. L.

FRIED POTATOES.

Cut into dice enough cold boiled potatoes to fill a pint
measure. Put a heaping tablespoon of butter in a hot
skillet. Pour in the potatoes. Add a half cup of cream
or milk. Put on a cover for five minutes. Salt and pepper. Serve in a hot dish.　　　　　　Mrs. E. E. W.

FRENCH FRIED POTATOES.

Pare small, raw potatoes. Divide into halves and cut each half into 3 pieces, lengthwise. Cook in boiling lard 10 minutes. Drain, salt, and serve hot.

Mrs. L. B. T.

KENTUCKY POTATOES.

The raw potatoes are sliced thin as for frying, and allowed to remain in cold water half an hour. The slices are then put into a pudding dish with salt, pepper and some milk—about half a pint to an ordinary dish. Bake half an hour. When taken from the oven a lump of butter half the size of an egg is cut into small bits and scattered over the top. The soaking in cold water hardens the slices so they keep their shape. The quantity of milk can only be leared by experience; if a little is left as a gravy moistening the slices it is right.

Mrs. A. G. C.

STUFFED POTATOES.

Take large fair potatoes, bake until soft. Cut into lengthways. Scrape out the inside, mash the potato smooth, adding butter, cream, salt and pepper. Fill the skins with the mixture. Beat the whites of 2 eggs, spread a spoonful over each potato case. Bake in a very slow oven 45 minutes. Serve hot. Mrs. M. G. T.

CREAMED POTATOES.

Slice cold boiled potatoes. Put over the fire with a generous covering of sweet milk, a large lump of butter, salt and pepper. As it boils chop into tiny bits with a sharp knife. Do not let boil too dry.

Mrs. M. F. V. R.

A DISH OF POTATOES AND CODFISH.

A pint bowl of salt codfish picked very fine; 2 pints potatoes cut up. Put both together and boil until thoroughly done. Drain off the water well, mash with a potato-masher, add a piece of butter the size of an egg, 2 well-beaten eggs, and a dash of pepper. Do not soak the fish, but wash well. Drop from spoon into hot lard. The mixture will take the form of crouquettes. The lard must be much hotter than for fried cakes. Garnish with celery-tops or parsley. Mrs. E. E. W.

POTATO PUFFS.

Take cold mashed potatoes, add the beaten white of an egg, butter and salt. Roll into balls the size of an egg. Dip in the yolk of the egg, lay on a buttered pan, bake until a light brown. Serve hot. Mrs. S. T. L.

POTATO OYSTER PATS.

Peel and boil 12 potatoes. Mash fine, salt to taste, and add a piece of butter the size of an egg, 4 tablespoons sweet cream or milk. Beat lightly and when cold work into pats, putting 2 oysters into each pat. Dip in beaten egg and roll in cracker meal. Put a little lump of butter on the top of each. Bake a light brown in a quick oven. Mrs. E. E. W.

GLAZED POTATOES.

Parboil in the skins, peel quickly and lay in a pan in the oven. A crust will form on them in a short time. Baste with butter until they assume a golden brown. Salt while boiling. Mrs. E. E. W.

POTATO CROUQUETTES.

Pare, boil and mash 6 large potatoes. Add 1 heaping tablespoon butter, ⅔ cup of hot cream, beaten whites of 2 eggs, salt and pepper. Roll the mixture into shape. Dip in egg and crumbs and fry in lard.

Mrs. S. T. L.

ASPARAGUS.

Having tied it in small bunches, boil until tender. Serve on buttered toast with drawn butter, salt and pepper.

Mrs. S. C. W.

COLD SLAW.

Shave or chop half a head of cabbage and put in dish. A large coffee-cup, ¾ full of cream, a heaped tablespoon of sugar stirred in. Finish filling the cup with vinegar.

Mrs. S. E. S.

STEWED CELERY.

Cut the celery in sticks an inch long. Cover with boiling water and simmer until tender. Season well with salt. Pour off the water, add a pint of cream ; allow this to heat thoroughly and serve.

Mrs. L. B. T.

CORN CLYSTERS.

Shave from the ear as much corn as is needed for a meal. Add a little sweet milk, beat in an egg and a teaspoon of flour. Drop by spoonful into boiling lard ; turning over when brown on one side. When done spread with a little butter.

Mrs. S. C. W.

CORN PUDDING.

12 ears of corn, 3 eggs beaten separately, 2 tablespoons of melted butter, 1 tablespoon white sugar, 1

heaping teaspoon flour, 1 teaspoon salt, 1 teacup milk. Cover and bake half an hour.　　　　　MRS. L. G. W.

MACARONI.

Break the macaroni in pieces an inch long, and put them in a pan of boiling water slightly salted. Stew gently until tender. Drain, lay in a buttered dish alternate layers of macaroni and cheese, with cheese at the top. Sprinkle each layer of macaroni with pepper and bits of butter. When the dish is full pour in enough milk to nearly cover and bake until nearly dry.

MRS. N. M. A.

RICE CROQUETTES.

1½ cups of boiled rice, ½ cup milk, 1 egg, 1 tablespoon sugar, 1 of butter, ½ teaspoon salt, a little nutmeg. Put the milk over to boil, add the rice and seasoning. When it boils, add the beaten egg. Stir one minute, then take off and cool. When cold make into forms and roll in egg and crumbs, and drop in hot lard. Serve very hot.　　　　　MRS. S. T. L.

PARSNIP BALLS.

Mash 1 pt. parsnips. Add 2 tablespoons butter, 1 teaspoonful salt, a little pepper, 2 tablespoons milk or cream, 1 egg well beaten. Mix all the ingredients except the egg. Stir over the fire 5 minutes. Add the egg and set away to cool. When cold, roll into balls, dip in egg and crumbs and fry in hot lard.　　　MRS. S. T. L.

PEAS.

Cook the peas in enough water to cover them, until tender, then add a teaspoon of butter, a little sugar and salt; thicken with a teaspoonful of flour.

Mrs. M. F. V R.

SQUASH.

Cut in small pieces, boil until tender. Then put them in a stew-pan, having mashed any hard pieces, add sufficient cream to make a soft mush. Stew until thick, add pepper, salt and butter. Mrs. S. C. W.

SALSIFY.

Scrape well, cut into pieces an inch long, dropping into cold water as cut. Put into a stew-pan and boil until done, then pour off the water ; add a little milk, butter, salt and pepper. Mrs. S. C. W.

SCALLOPED TOMATOES.

Put a layer of tomatoes in an earthen dish, stew with salt and pepper and bits of butter. Cover with a layer of bread crumbs, then tomatoes, and so on until the dish is full, having crumbs for top layer. Bake half an hour. Mrs. S. T. L.

FRIED TOMATOES.

Pare large, solid tomatoes and slice in thick slices. Dip on both sides in flour, and fry in butter on a griddle. Mrs. S. T. L.

SALADS.

DELMONICO'S MAYONNAISE.

Yolks of 2 eggs, 1 teacup olive oil. Put the unbeaten yolks in a soup-plate and stir with a silver fork ; add the oil slowly, work to the consistency of butter. Take a cup with 2 tablespoons of vinegar, 1 teaspoon salt, 1 small teaspoon mixed mustard, ½ teaspoon white su-

gar, a pinch of pepper. Mix well then stir gently on
the dressing. Beat the whites of both eggs and use a
tablespoon of lemon juice in place of the vinegar.

MRS. A. S. B.

COOKED SALAD DRESSING.

Yolks of 4 eggs, a teaspoon of pepper, 2 tablespoons
of mustard, 1 of white sugar, 2 of vinegar, 4 of butter.
Cook over boiling water 3 minutes. When done add ½
cup more vinegar.   MRS S. R. M.

SALAD DRESSING.

Four eggs beaten together, only yolks will do; 1 tablespoon dry mustard, 1 cup vinegar, salt and pepper to
taste. Beat thoroughly and boil in a dish of water, stirring constantly. When done add ½ cup sour cream.

MRS. S. T. L.

POTATO SALAD.

Boil 6 or 7 large potatoes. When done peel, slice
fine and season with salt and pepper. Cut 1 onion fine
and put into a skillet in which a large tablespoon of
lard is hot—let onions cook, but not fry ; when done,
pour ½ pint of good vinegar and a ½ pint of water
mixed into skillet, and let come to a boil. Then pour
all over potatoes and mix thoroughly. Prepared a short
time before the meal improves it.   Mrs. J. L. N.

CHICKEN SALAD.

Two large chickens boiled tender. When cold, chop
fine. Chop cabbage equal in amount to chicken. Mix
thoroughly and sprinkle with a teaspoon of salt, and a
tablespoon of celery seed. Beat the yolks of 6 eggs, a
little, add to them a small teaspoon of pepper, butter the

size of a walnut, a teaspoon of white sugar, a heaping
tablespoon of mustard mixed to a smooth paste with a
of tumbler of strong vinegar. Cook all in a double kettle, stirring constantly, until a thick paste. When perfectly cold pour over the chicken and add a tumbler of
chopped pickle. Mix well.   Mrs. M. W. W.

PICKLES, CATSUPS.

GREEN CUCUMBER PICKLE.

Green the cucumbers in vinegar and water, half and
half, with a piece of alum the size of a walnut. Cover
while greening with grape leaves. Peel and slice the
onions, scald with boiling water. 3 gals. cucumbers, 12
large onions, 1 1-2 gals. cider vinegar, 2 tablespoons
each of black mustard seed, white mustard seed, ground
ginger, ground mace, celery seed, cinnamon, turmerac,
4 lbs. brown sugar. Stir the sugar and spices in the
boiling vinegar and pour over the cucumbers and onions,
mixed in jars.   Mrs. W. H. C.

SLICED CUCUMBER PICKLE.

Peel and slice thin, large cucumbers, sprinkle over
a little salt, stand 24 hours. Drain off water thoroughly, if too salt wash before putting in vinegar. Slice as
many onions as for ordinary cucumbers. Pour boiling
salt water on the onions and let them stand half an hour.
Drain mix with the cucumbers. Put in porcelain kettle enough cider vinegar to cover them. Add a little

brown sugar, ground pepper, celery seed and white mustard seed. When it boils add onions and cucumbers. As soon as hot pour into jars and seal.   Mrs. R. T.

NEW SPANISH PICKLE.

3 dozen cucumbers, 2 large cabbage heads, chopped fine, half gallon onion, cut into small squares, cucumbers also cut into squares. Salt and let stand one hour. Scald all in vinegar, then season with horseradish, one box Lexington mustard, one oz. celery seed, one oz. tumerac, one lb. sugar, 2 ozs. white mustard seed, ten pods of pepper.   Mrs. J. H. M'H.

MUSTARD PICKLE.

One and a half gals. chopped cucumbers, a handful of salt. Stand 24 hours. Press out the salt water, boil until very tender in fresh water. Drain dry. Slice six small onions, boil until tender, and mix with cucumbers. To this add 20 cents' worth of mustard, 10 of ginger, 5 of tumerac, one teaspoon of pepper, 2 tablespoons olive oil. Cover with vinegar and let come to a boil.

Miss S. R. M.

SWEET CHOPPED PICKLE.

8 lbs. green tomatoes, chop fine, add 4 lbs. brown sugar; boil 3 hours. Add a qt. of vinegar, 1 teaspoon each of mace, cinnamon and cloves. Boil 15 minutes; when cool put in jars.   Mrs. A. G. C.

WATERMELON PICKLE.

Peel and cut in small, narrow pieces the rind of 2 medium size melons. Let stand over night in strong ginger tea of unground ginger, boil the melon in this until tender. Put enough vinegar to cover over the fire, adding 1 lb. sugar to each pint of vinegar, 2 tablespoons white mustard seed, ¼ ib. stick cinnamon and some of the ginger tea. When this boils, add the fruit and boil 1 hour.

Mrs. A. S. B.

DAMSON SWEET PICKLE.

Perforate the skins of 9 pts. of Damsons. 3 pts. vinegar, 4 lbs. brown sugar and pour on the fruit. Let them stand 24 hours. Pour off the vinegar, boil, and pour on the fruit. Do this 4 days. The fourth day add cinnamon and spices. Boil until the syrup is as thick as molasses. Peaches or pears may be pickled in the same manner.

Mrs. S. C. W.

GRAPE PICKLE.

Pack the grapes, on the stems, in jars. Make a syrup of 5 lbs. sugar to 1 qt. vinegar. Add mace and cinnamon to taste. Boil the syrup until thick, pour over the grapes and seal.

Mrs. A. S. B.

TOMATO CATSUP.

Ten qts. of tomato pulp strained through a colander, 2 qts. vinegar, 5 tablespoons black pepper, 3 of white ginger, 4 of grated horseradish, 4 of English mustard, 2 of cloves, 2 of allspice, 3 of celery seed, 3 of grated nutmeg. Six grated onions, 4 teacups brown sugar, salt to taste. boil till thick, and bottle.

Mrs. M. W. W.

PIES.

MINCE PIES.

One and a half lbs. heart or tongue, 2 lbs. beef suet, 4 lbs. pippin apples, 2 lbs. raisins, 2 lbs. currants, 2 lbs. citron, 2 lbs. sugar, 2 large oranges. 1 qt. white wine, 1 qt. brandy, wine-glass rose water, 2 grated nutmegs, 1 ½ ozs. cloves, cinnamon and mace, 1 teaspoon salt. Parboil the meat (it must weigh 1¼ lbs. without skin or fat.) When cold chop very fine. Mix with the chopped suet, adding the salt. Add the chopped apples, chopped raisins and other fruit. Then the sugar, spices, peel and juice of the oranges, rose-water and liquor. Mix all well.   Mrs. M. A. T.

PUMPKIN PIES.

Pare the pumpkin, cut into pieces an inch square. Put over the fire with very little water. As it begins to get soft, put over a slow fire, and stir frequently to prevent burning, for it must cook until all the water has evaporated. Then rub through a colander, and it is ready for use. For 4 pies, take 3 pints of sweet milk, 6 eggs, 1 small nutmeg, 1 teaspoon of cinnamon, 2 tablespoons of butter, a little salt. Beat the eggs, add the milk, spices, salt and the butter melted, then add sugar until quite sweet, and enough of the stewed pumpkin to make it the consistency of boiled custard.   Mrs. M. F. V R.

SWEET POTATO PIE.

Boil 3 large sweet potatoes. When done peel and slice thin. To this add 2 cups sweet preserves, 1 cup sugar, 1 cup butter, 1 teaspoon cloves, 1 teaspoon all-spice, a little nutmeg. Bake with a top crust. This makes 2 large pies, usually made in pudding dishes.

MRS. J. L. N

MOLASSES PIES.

Two eggs, half-pint of molasses, two tablespoons of butter, one nutmeg. Beat well the eggs, add the molasses and melted butter, then the nutmeg. Roll the pastry thin, and line two tins, then pour in the mixture.

MISS M. V R.

FRENCH CREAM PIE.

Three eggs, one cup white sugar, one and a half cups flour, 1 teaspoon Cleveland's Superior Baking Powder, two tablespoons cold water. Split while warm and spread with cream filling. *Cream:* Boil 1 pt. sweet milk. To this add when boiling, 2 small tablespoons corn starch beaten in milk, mixed with two eggs, 1 scant cup sugar. When nearly done add half cup butter and two table-spoons vanilla. Sprinkle the top with sugar and grated cocoanut.

MRS. J. B. S.

COCOANUT PIE.

Grate a cocoanut. Boil a qt. of rich milk, pour upon it; add 4 eggs beaten very light, with a coffee-cup of sugar, a tablespoon of melted butter, half teaspoon of salt, a little cinnamon. Line two deep plates with pie-crust. Bake till firm.

MRS. L. B. T.

PEACH MERINGUE PIE.

Line a pie-plate with pastry, and bake. Pare and halve

ten peaches, stew until tender in a cup of water and one of sugar. Lay the peaches on the pastry, thicken the syrup with a tablespoon of flour and pour over the peaches. On each piece of fruit place a teaspoon of meringue, prepared by beating the white of an egg with a tablespoon of sugar: Bake until a light brown.

Mrs. L. B. T.

GRAPE PIE.

Fill a pie-crust with fresh grapes, washed and picked from the stem. Bake half an hour. When done pour over it a batter of eggs, 1 cup sugar, 1 cup flour, two tablespoons water, two teaspoons Cleveland's Superior Baking Powder. Brown in the oven enough for two pies.

Mrs. C. J. Q.

TRANSPARENT PIES.

One large cup of sugar, one small cup of butter, 8 eggs, 1 lemon, juice and peel. Cream the butter and sugar, add the yolks of the eggs and then the lemon. This makes 3 large pies. Make a meringue of the whites and spread over the pies when done. Put back in the oven until slightly browned.

MISS M. V R.

CHESS CAKE.

Yolks 8 eggs, one-half lb. butter, one-half lb. sugar. Beat well, put over the fire and thicken. Bake on thin pastry. Makes 3 pies.

Mrs. M. W. W.

DESERTS.

PLUM PUDEING.

Half lb. raisins, half lb. currants, ¼ lb. citron, sprinkle with a little flour; 6 eggs, beaten separately; half lb. flour, half lb. sugar, scant ¼ lb. butter, half lb. suet, a little salt, scant half pint milk, in which soak two slices baker's bread. Mix the whites and yolks, add sugar and butter, stir in suet, milk and flour, one nutmeg mixed in a teaspoon of brandy. Add the fruit and boil four hours.   Mrs. B. W. G.

JEFF DAVIS PUDDING.

Three cups sugar, 1 cup molasses, 1 cup beef suet chopped fine, 1 cup sour cream, 1 cup raisins, seeded and split open; put in at the last a little salt.
                    Mrs. M. W. W.

FRUIT PUDDING.

One cup butter, 1 cup sugar, 2 cups flour, yolks 4 eggs, 4 tablespoons sour cream, 1 teaspoon soda, 1½ cups of jam or cherries, or 1 cup raisins and half a cup of currants. Bake one hour. Beat the whites of the eggs to a stiff froth, spread over the top, return to the oven and brown slightly. To be eaten with sweet sauce.
                    Mrs. M. F. V R.

CHOCOLATE PUDDING.

Two eggs, 7 tablespoons sugar, 1 tablespoon butter, 1 small cup milk or cream. When the pudding is nearly done spread with a meringue of egg, sugar and vanilla. Set in the oven to harden. Bake in a rich puff paste.
                    Mrs. B. W. G.

LEMON PUDDING

Seven eggs, 3 lemons, 3 teacups white sugar, 1 lb. butter. Use half the whites for the icing. Beat the yolks and sugar together, add the lemon juice with the grated peel of two lemons and half a nutmeg. Beat half the whites well, mix with the butter, sugar and lemons. Bake on a rich thin pastry. When done put on the icing and brown.   Mrs. M W. W.

BLACK PUDDING.

One pt. molasses, 1 pt. blackberry jam, 1 teacup buttermilk, 1 teaspoon soda, 1 of nutmeg and 1 of cinnamon, enough flour to make a stiff batter. Steam or bake.   Mrs. S. E. S.

FIG PUDDING.

½ lb. figs, chopped fine ; 6 oz. sugar, 6 oz. suet, ¾ lbs. bread crumbs, 2 eggs, 1 teacup milk, ½ teaspoon soda, a little salt. Steam 3 hours.   Mrs. M. R. B.

GINGER PUDDING.

One cup molasses, 1 cup brown sugar, 1 cup lard, 1 teaspoon ginger, 2 teaspoons soda, 3 eggs beaten separately, flour to make as stiff as cake. Bake quickly.
                                                Mrs. L. G. W.

MARCH PUDDING.

One cup dried apples, 1 egg, 1 cup molasses, 1¼ cups flour, ¼ cup butter, ¼ teaspoon cloves, 1 teaspoon soda, 1 teaspoon cinnamon. Wash and soak the apples over night. Cut fine and add the other ingredients, and bake at once. Serve hot with a sauce of half cup butter and 1 cup sugar beaten smooth and flavored.
                                                Mrs. L. B. T.

WHITE STEAMED PUDDING.

One cup sweet milk, half cup sugar, 1 egg, half tea-spoon soda, 1 cream tartar, butter size of half egg, 2⅓ cups flour. Steam one and a half hours. Is delicious with raisins or fruit.   Mrs. L. B. T.

APPLE-BATTER PUDDING.

6 or 8 large apples, 1 qt. sweet milk, 10 large table-spoons of flour, 4 eggs, 1 spoon Cleveland's Superior Baking Powder in the flour, a pinch of salt. Pare and core the apples and steam until tender, but not enough to break. Then peel in a baking dish and pour over them a batter made by beating the eggs well and adding the milk and salt. Then stiffen with the flour. Bake thirty minutes and serve immediately with sauce.

Peach batter pudding is made in the same way, unless the peaches are very ripe, when they need not be steamed.

Mrs. M. F. V R.

CREAM RICE PUDDING.

¼ cup rice, half cup sugar, 1 qt. sweet milk. Put in pudding dish with bits of butter over the top. Flavor with nutmeg. Bake slowly until the rice is cooked, then stir in a tablespoon of corn starch dissolved in a little milk. It will then have the consistency of cream. If too thick add a little milk. Serve hot or cold.

Mrs. N. M. A.

TAPIOCA PUDDING.

1 cup tapioca soaked over night. Grate 2 large apples and 1 lemon, 1 cup sugar, 1 tablespoon butter. Place on stove and boil. When taken off add 3 well beaten eggs. Serve with whipped cream.   Miss L. N.

SPONGE CAKE PUDDING:

3 eggs, 1 cup sugar, beat with two tablespoons water,

1 cup flour, two teaspoons Cleveland's Superior Baking Powder. Bake in two layers. *Filling:* Beat 1 egg, and half cup sugar, ¼ cup flour, wet with a little milk. Stir this mixture into half pt. boiling milk. When thick, flavor and spread between the layers. Eat with lemon sauce.   Mrs. C. J. Q.

SUNDERLAND PUDDING.

One pt. milk, 4 eggs beaten separately, 3 tablespoons flour, a little salt. Beat yolks, add flour and milk, then whites. Bake in a well-greased pudding dish about 20 minutes, or until set like a custard. Serve the moment it comes from the oven, with hot sauce.

Mrs L. B. T.

PEACH COBBLER.

Stew and sweeten the peaches, bake in a pudding dish with upper and lower crust. Before serving, raise the crust and pour in some cream and butter. A good way to make cobbler, is to roll pastry in sheets the same size and bake. Pile it with fruit, in layers. On top lay some slender strips of pastry, sprinkle with sugar and serve with cream.   Mrs. B. W. G.

PRUNE SOUFFLE.

Cook ¾ lbs. of prunes until tender, chop fine. Beat the whites of 5 eggs to a stiff froth, with 10 tablespoons sugar, Add 2 tablespoons chopped prunes. Pour into a well-greased pudding dish, cover with a colander and bake in a moderate oven 20 minutes. Serve at once with cold cream. Care must be taken not to disturb the pudding while baking. The dish should not be more than two-thirds full when put in the oven, as the eggs rise.   Mrs. C. G.

CHOCOLATE MERINGUE.

Ten cents' worth of shelled almonds, 5 of sweet choco-late, 1 teacup rolled crackers, 1 lemon, juice and rind ; 2 tablespoons cinnamon, 1 of cloves, 1 of allspice, 2 cups powdered sugar, 6 eggs. Flavor. Two teaspoons Cleveland's Superior Baking Powder. Bake. Then spread on fruit jelly and frosting and bake until a light brown. MRS. J. H. M'H.

CREAM SAUCE.

Half cup butter, 1 cup powdered sugar, ¼ cup cream, 1 teaspoon vanilla. Beat the butter to a cream, add the sugar, stirring constantly, then the flavoring and cream, slowly. When smooth set in hot water and cook until creamy. MRS. B. W. G.

SAUCE.

Boil 1 cup of sugar and 1 cup of water 3 or 4 minutes, then stir in 1 tablespoon of butter well mixed with one tablespoon of flour. Remove from the fire for a few minutes, and stir in the yolk of 1 egg well beaten.

MISS .M. V R.

LEMON SAUCE.

One cup sugar, ½ cup butter, creamed. Add the yolks of 2 eggs and 1 pt. boiling water, with the juice of a lemon, then the beaten whites. MRS. S. T. L.

EGG SAUCE

One cup sugar beaten with 2 eggs, 1 heaping table-spoon butter. Cook and serve hot. MRS. S. T. L.

CHARLOTTE RUSSE.

One qt. cream, 1 teaspoon vanilla, ¾ cup granulated

sugar, ½ pack Chalmer's gelatine, lady fingers. In using Aidnery cream, mix with milk. Line the mo'ds with lady fingers. Soak the gelatine in half cup cold milk. Whip the cream to a stiff froth; set the bowl in a dish of ice-water. Sprinkle over the cream, the sugar and vanilla. Pour ½ cup boiling milk or water over the soaked gelatine. When well dissolved, strain. Stir gently until it begins to thicken, and add the cream from the top. When it will just pour, fill the molds and set away on ice. Mrs. S A. V.

RUSSIAN CREAM.

Dissolve half box Chalmer's gelatine in ½ cup cold water. Put over 1 qt. milk, when hot, add the gelatine, yolks of 4 eggs beaten with 1 teacup sugar. Cook until a custard, remove from the fire, add the beaten whites and 1 teaspoon vanilla. Pour into molds. Serve with cream. Mrs. S. T. L.

ITALIAN CREAM.

One qt. cream whipped, 1 oz. Chalmer's gelatine dissolved in ½ pt. hot water, 1 teacup sugar; flavor to taste. Mrs. S. T. L.

SNOW-BALL PUDDING.

Half box Chalmer's gelatine dissolved in 1 pt. boiling water, 2 cups granulated sugar, juice 2 lemons; strain and cook. When quite thick add whites 3 eggs beaten stiff. Beat all together till a white froth; let it harden in cups. Make a custard with 3 yolks, 1 whole egg, 1½ pts. milk; flavor with vanilla. Pour into a glass dish. When cold lay the balls on the custard. Mrs. L. B. T.

LEMON SPONGE.

To 1 oz. Chalmer's gelatine add 1 pt. cold water. Let it stand 5 minutes, then dissolve over the fire. Add the rind of 2 lemons and the juice of 3, with ¾ lbs. white sugar. Boil 2 minutes, strain, and let stand until nearly cold. Add the whites of 2 eggs beaten stiff. Whip all until the consistency of sponge. Mrs. M. R. B.

COFFEE JELLY.

1 qt. strong coffee. Sweeten to suit the taste ; settle, and strain perfectly clear. Dissolve half box Chalmer's gelatine in half cup boiling water, add to the coffee. Pour in molds wet with cold water. Serve with whipped cream. Mrs S. T. L.

CUSTARD.

12 eggs, 4 qts. new milk, 1 pt. white sugar. Put sugar in the milk, beat the eggs together. When milk boils, pour on the beaten eggs. Return to the fire and stir until it begins to thicken. Cook in a dish with water around it. Mrs. L. G. W.

VANILLA ICE-CREAM.

1 pt milk, 1 cup sugar, scant ½ cup flour, 2 eggs, 1 qt. cream, 1 tablespoon vanilla. Let the milk come to a boil, add the sugar and flour, well mixed together, then the well-beaten eggs. Cook until a rich custard. When cold add the cream, flavoring, and another cup of sugar. Mrs. S. T. L.

STRAWBERRY ICE-CREAM.

2 qts. berries, mashed smooth ; 2 qts. cream. Whip the cream well, add the berries, make very sweet and freeze. Mrs. L. G. W.

LEMON SHERBET.

To each can of pineapple add juice of 4 lemons and 1 qt. of water. Whites of 3 eggs; make rather sweet and freeze.   Mrs. L. G. W.

ORANGE SHERBET.

1 qt. water, 1 pt. sugar, juice of 4 oranges and 3 lemons, whites of 2 eggs beaten to a stiff froth, stirred in just before freezing.   Mrs. S. A. V.

JUNKET.

Take one-half pint fresh milk, heated as hot as can be agreeably borne by the mouth (about 115° F.), add 1 teaspoonful of Fairchild Bros. & Foster's Essence of Pepsine, and stir just enough to mix. Let it stand till firmly curded; may be served plain or with sugar and grated nutmeg.

WHEY.

Curd warm milk with Essence of Pepsine, as above directed. When firmly curded beat up with a fork until the curd is finely divided. Now strain and the whey is ready for use.

Whey is a highly nutritious fluid food, containing in solution the sugar and the salts (the mineral constituents) of the milk, and holding also in suspension a considerable portion of caseine and fat (cream) which pass through the strainer. It is peculiarly useful in many ailments and always valuable as a means of variety in diet for the sick. It is frequently resorted to as a food for infants to tide over periods of indigestion, summer complaints, etc.

CAKES, ICING, COOKIES, ETC.

FRUIT CAKE.

1 lb. flour, 1 lb. sugar. 1 heavy lb. butter, 2½ lbs. raisins, 1 lb. citron, 1½ lbs. currants, 1 doz. eggs, 2 nutmegs. 1 tablespoon ground cloves, 1 oz. ground ginger, 1 gill brandy. Cream the butter and sugar. Whip the eggs and pour into the sugar and butter. Then add the flour. Cut the fruit, mix alternate handful into the batter; put in spices and brandy last. Bake 3 hours in a moderate oven.   Mrs. M. A. T.

CURRANT BUN.

Seed 2 lbs. raisins, 2 lbs. Sultana raisins, 2 lbs. currants, 1 lb. blanched almonds, ¾ lb. orange peel, ¼ lb. citron peel, 1 nutmegs, 1 lb. sugar, 6 oz. butter, 4 lbs. breap dough; ½ oz. ground carraway seed, 1 oz. ground ginger, ½ oz. ground cinnamon, half oz. ground corriander seeds. Make a hole in the dough, put in the butter and set before the fire until it melts; then jwork in well. Keep out ⅓ the dough, mix the fruit in the rest; press into the pan, turn out, and press with the hands a little, all around. Line the pan with the remaining dough, put in the fruit mixture, and cover with the dough. Bake in a bread oven 3 hours.   Mrs. M. R. B.

NUT CAKE.

1 cup butter, 2 cups sugar, 1 cup sweet milk, 4 cups flour, whites 6 eggs, 1 heaping teaspoon Cleveland's Superior Baking Powder, 2 cups pecan kernels.

                                          Mrs. N. M. A.

COFFEE CAKE.

2 eggs, 2 cups clear coffee, 1 pt. raisins, 1 pt. currants, 1 tablespoon cinnamon, 1-2 tablespoon cloves, 1 nutmeg, 1 even tablespoon soda, ¾ cup butter, 3 1-2 cups flour.   Mrs. A. S. B.

GINGERBREAD.

1 lb. flour, 1 pt. N. O. molasses, 1 teacup hot water, 2 1-2 teaspoons ginger, 1 of cinnamon, 5 oz. butter.

Mrs. S. D.

LEMON POUND CAKE.

1 lb. flour, 1 lb. sugar, ¾ lb. butter, 7 eggs, juice of 2 lemons.   Miss L. N.

WHITE CAKE.

1 cup butter, 2 cups sugar, 4 cups flour, 1 cup sweet milk, whites of 8 eggs, 2 teaspoons Cleveland's Superior Baking Powder.   Mrs. J. R. W.

SPONGE CAKE.

12 eggs, 1¾ pints sugar, 1¾ pints sifted flour. Beat whites of the eggs to a stiff froth. Into the well-beaten yolks, gradually stir the sugar and then the beaten whites. Remove your spoon from this mixture and with a large knife cut in the sifted flour. Never stir it after putting in the flour.   Mrs. S. A. V.

ROLL JELLY CAKE.

One cup sugar, 2 eggs, well beaten, 2 tablespoons water. Mix 1 1-2 teaspoons Cleveland's Superior Baking Powder in 1 1-2 cups flour. Stir a very little after adding the flour. Flavor to taste. Bake in a dripping pan in a *quick* oven. Spread with jelly, roll and slice.

Mrs. C. J. Q.

PRINCE ALBERT CAKE.

White. Whites 4 eggs, 2 cups sugar, 1 cup sweet milk, 1 cup butter, 3 cups flour, 1 teaspoon Cleveland's Superior Baking Powder.

Dark. 1 cup brown sugar, 3 eggs, half cup milk or cream, half cup butter, 1½ cups stoned raisins, 2 cups flour, half teaspoon Cleveland's Superior Baking Powder, 1 teaspoon cloves, cinnamon and allspice. Bake in long pans: put icing between. Mrs M. W. W.

BLACK CHOCOLATE CAKE.

1 cup butter, 2 cups sugar, 5 eggs, whites of 2, 1 cup milk, 2 teaspoons Cleveland's Superior Baking Powder, half cake chocolate.

Filling. 1 lb. sugar wet with cold water, 1 cup cocoanut, whites 3 eggs, half cake chocolate. Cook over water, stirring constantly. MRS. L. B. T.

BROWN STONE FRONT CAKE.

Whites of 4 eggs, 1 cup milk, half cup butter, 2 cups sugar, 3 cups flour, 3 teaspoons Cleveland's Superior Baking Powder. Make a paste of half cake chocolate, half cup milk, 1 cup sugar, yolk of 1 egg. Boil until a thick caromel. When nearly cold stir into the cake. Bake in 4 layers and put together with boiled frosting.

MRS. S. T. L.

COCOANUT CAKE.

2 cups sugar, half cup butter, 3 eggs, 1 cup milk, 3 cups flour, 3 teaspoons Cleveland's Superior Baking Powder. Flavor to taste. Cream the butter and sugar, add the eggs, mix quick with the milk, then pour into

the butter and sugar and eggs : add the flour. The batter must be so thick that it has to be spread in the pans with a knife. Bake very quickly in a hot oven without allowing time to brown. *Filling :* Whites 4 eggs, half cup sugar, 1 ground cocoanut. Spread the top with icing and sprinkle on cocoanut.   Mrs. M. W. W.

CREAM CAKE.

3 eggs, 1 cup sugar, 2 tablespoons cold water, 1½ cups flour, 1 teaspoon flavoring. Bake in 2 jelly pans. *Cream:* Let 1 pint milk come to a boil, then add 1 cup sugar, 2 eggs, and a small piece butter, beaten together. Let all come to a boil. Do not allow it to boil or it will curdle. Pour out and when cool, flavor. Split the cakes in half and spread the filling between.   Mrs. H. W.

ICE CREAM CAKE.

2 cups white sugar, 1 cup butter, 1 cup sweet milk, whites 8 eggs, 2 teaspoons Cleveland's Superior Baking Powder, 3½ cups flour. Bake in layers. *Filling:* 3 cups sugar, 1 cup water, boil to a thick syrup ; pour the boiling syrup over the whites of 3 eggs, well beaten ; add a teaspoon powdered citric acid, flavor with lemon or vanilla : spread on each layer.   Mrs. H. W.

WHITE CAROMEL CAKE.

Whites of 10 eggs, 2½ cups sugar, 1 cup butter, 1 cup milk, 4 cups flour, 3 teaspoons Cleveland's Superior Baking Powder. *Filling:* 3 cups white sugar, 1½ cups cream, 1 cup butter. Boil until it candies, stirring constantly.   Mrs. M. W. W.

MARSH-MALLOW CAKE.

Three cups sugar, 1½ cups butter, 5 cups flour, 1 cup

sweet milk, the whites of 12 eggs, 2 teaspoons Cleveland's Superior Baking Powder. Cream the butter and sugar, then add the milk slowly, then half the eggs and half the flour : the other half the eggs and the rest of the flour into which first stir the baking powder. Bake in layers, spread icing between and split the mash-mallows and lay them on very closely together. Ice the top and lay on whole marsh-mallows. One and a half lbs. marsh-mallows will be required. Miss M. V. R.

ICING.

Whites 2 eggs, 1 tablespoon vinegar or lemon juice, 1 teaspoon starch, thicken with sugar. Wrap a silver fork with cloth : stir the above. Mrs. M. W. W.

LEMON FILLING.

Juice and grated rind of 3 lemons, 1 cup sugar, 1 cup butter, 3 eggs. Beat the eggs, stir in lemon, sugar and butter. Cook until thick, stirring constantly.

Miss S. R. M.

COCOANUT FILLING.

Whip 1 pint cream, sweeten and flavor with vanilla. Into this stir lightly a grated cocoanut. Miss M. V R.

ALMOND FILLING.

Whites 3 beaten eggs, 2 small cups powdered sugar, half cup almonds, blanched and powdered fine : stir into the icing. Flavor with rose-water or bitter almond. This is very nice made of whipped cream instead of eggs. Miss M. V R.

GINGER SNAPS.

One and a half cups molasses, 1 cup brown sugar, 1

large cup lard, 1 tablespoon soda. Cinnamon and salt.
Boil 15 minutes. When cold mix stiff with flour, roll
very thin and bake in a quick oven.   Mrs. S. T. L.

HARD GINGER CAKES.

6 pints flour, 1 ℔. sugar, 1 pt. molasses, 5 tablespoons
ginger, 1 teaspoon soda, 1 ℔. lard, 6 tablespoons buttermilk. Roll thin and bake quickly.   Mrs. M. R. B.

SOFT GINGER CAKES.

1 heaping cup butter, 1 large cup sugar, 1 pt. molasses, half pt. milk, 1 oz. soda, 1 oz. cinnamon, 1 nutmeg.
Bake in a dripping pan; when nearly cold, cut in
squares.   ·   Mrs. L. B. T.

CINNAMON CAKES.

1 ℔. butter 2 ℔s. flour, 1 ℔. brown sugar, yolks 6 eggs.
Make a thin icing. Roll the cakes thin, spreading with
the icing; sift on cinnamon. Before quite dry sift over
with powdered sugar.   Mrs. R. T.

SAND TARTS.

2 eggs well beaten, half teaspoon soda, 3 tablespoons
water, flour to roll thin. Sprinkle on top with sugar,
cinnamon, raisins or almonds. Bake in a hot oven.
    Mrs. B. W. G.

TEA CAKES.

4 eggs, two and a half cups sugar, ⅔ cup butter, 3
teaspoons Cleveland's Superior Baking Powder. Flavor
to taste and flour enough to roll well.   Mrs. J. W. R.

FRIED CAKES.

3 eggs, 2 cups sugar, 1 pt. sweet milk, 1 heaping ta-

blespoon butter, 1 teaspoon sait, one and a half table
spoons vanilla, 4 teaspoons Cleveland's Superior Baking
Powder, sifted with the flour. Mix soft. Cream butter
and sugar, add yolks of eggs, butter and vanilla. Add
beaten whites with the flour, last.   Mrs. L. B. T.

PRESERVES, JELLIES.

PRESERVED STRAWBERRIES,

To 1 lb. of berries use ¾ lb. of sugar, in layers.
Place in a kettle on back of the stove until the sugar
dissolves, then let it come to a boil, stirring from the
bottom. Spread on plates and set in the sun until the
syrup thickens. It may require two or three days. Pour
into cans and seal.   Mrs. L. B. T.

RASPBERRY AND CURRANT PRESERVES,

Take ⅔ red raspberries and ⅓ of currants. Weigh
them, put a pound of sugar to a pound of fruit, and
let them boil 20 minutes, or until the syrup begins to
jelly.   Mrs. M. F. V R.

PEAR PRESERVES.

Pare and quarter the pears, weigh, and if hard, boil in
a little water until soft before adding the sugar, pound
for pound. When nearly done add a sliced lemon to
every four pounds of fruit. Cook until the syrup when
cold forms a thin jelly.   Mrs. M. F. V R.

QUINCE MARMALADE,

Pare and cut the fruit fine. Boil the corings and par-
ings, then strain and add the quinces Let them boil

until soft : mash fine and add ¾ ℔. sugar to 1 ℔. fruit
Cook gently 2 hours or until a thick jam.

Mrs. R. T.

PINE APPLE MARMALADE.

Pare and chop the pines. To 1 lb. fruit add 1½ lbs.
granulated sugar. Place in an earthen dish and stand
in a cool place for 24 hours. Heat thoroughly and can.

Mrs. S. T. L.

GOOSEBERRY JELLY.

To each gallon of well-grown, but not ripe berries, allow 3 pts. water. Boil until tender. Pour into a flan-
nel bag to drip. To each pt. of juice allow 1 lb. of sugar. Boil quickly until it will jelly.   Mrs. S. C. W.

LEMON FRUIT JELLY.

Make a rich lemonade of the juice of 6 large lemons,
2 cups sugar, 1½ qts. water. Add small slices of citron
and the yellow part of lemon and orange peel. Heat,
and add 1 box Chalmer's gelatine, already dissolved in 1
pt. water. Pour one-third the preparation into moulds:
arrange slices of orange, bananas and pineapple in it
and let it partially form, add another third and arrange fruit as in the first. Then pour in the remainder
and let stand on ice over night. In very hot weather a
little more gelatine is required. When removing from
the moulds, dip in hot water only an instant, as it melts
rapidly.   Mrs. A. C. S.

PINEAPPLE JELLY.

1 box Chalmer's gelatine, 1 can grated pineapple, juice
3 lemons, sugar enough to sweeten. Soak the gelatine
an hour in 1 pt. cold water. Add 1 pt. boiling water,
then the lemon juice and pineapple.   Miss M. V R.

DRINKS.

COFFEE.

1 small teacup coffee, 1 qt. fresh cold water. Boil the coffee 3 minutes, then set it where it will keep warm until ready for use. MRS. L. G. W.

CHOCOLATE.

Dissolve ½ cake Baker's chocolate in 1 qt. boiling water. Boil rapidly, stirring constantly, 5 minutes. Add ½ cup sugar, and 1 qt. hot milk When the mixture begins to boil stir in a heaping teaspoon of corn starch, previously dissolved in cold milk. Boil for a minute, remove from the fire and add a teaspoon of vanilla. Serve with whipped cream. MRS. S. T. L.

STRAWBERRY ACID.

Dissolve 5 ozs. tartaric acid in 1 pt. water and pour over 12 lbs. sugar. Let stand 24 hours and add 12 qts. strawberry juice. Bottle. MRS. R. T.

RASPBERRY VINEGAR.

To 8 qts. berries add 4 qts. vinegar. Let stand 48 hours. Strain, and to every quart of juice allow ¾ lb. sugar, boil 10 minutes and bottle. MRS. S. T. L.

BLACKBERRY CORDIAL.

Select coarse-grain, well-ripened berries. To each gal. allow 3 pts. water. Boil in a porcelain kettle. When soft, strain out the seeds and pulp. To each gal. of the liquid add 3 lbs. lump sugar, 3 sticks cinnamon

2 doz. cloves, a large tablespoon allspice. Boil 10 minutes. When cold strain out the spices and stir in 1 qt.
old whiskey.   Mrs. S. C. W.

UNFERMENTED WINE.

Mash the grapes, and boil or not, as convenient ; by
boiling more color is extracted from the skins. Strain
the juice, sweeten to taste, fill the bottles and set on a
firm foundation in a big kettle with water to the neck
of the bottles. Allow the water to boil 10 minutes.
Refill the bottles, cork and seal while hot. Poured on
ice and water it makes a most refreshing drink ; no
headache in it.   Mrs. L. G. W.

CANDIES.

MOLASSES CANDY.

2 cups molasses, 1 cup sugar, 1 tablespoon vinegar, a
small piece of butter. Boil until brittle. Before taking from the stove add a little soda.   Miss U. R. T.

BUTTER SCOTCH.

1 cup brown sugar, 1 cup N. O. molasses, ½ cup butter. Boil until crisp. Pour on buttered tins and mark
in squares.   Mrs. B. W. G.

CREAM CANDY.

2½ cups sugar, ½ cup boiling water, 2 teaspoons vinegar, butter size of a hickory nut. Boil 15 minutes
without stirring.   Miss U. R. T.

BROWN SUGAR CANDY.

3 lbs. sugar, ½ cup boiling water, 2 teaspoons vinegar, a large tablespoon butter. Boil without stirring. Pull with the ends of the fingers, when cool.

Mrs. S. C. W.

CHOCOLATE CARAMELS.

½ lb. butter, 3 lbs. N. O. brown sugar, ½ lb. Baker's chocolate, ½ pt. morning's milk. Stir often. When done add ½ oz. vanilla, pour on greased pans and cut in squares.

Mrs. B. W. G.

COCOANUT CANDY.

2 lbs. sugar, the milk from the cocoanut with enough water added to make a pint. Let it boil, without stirring, until brittle in water. Pour over the grated cocoanut and beat until it thickens, then drop in small cakes or pour in pans and cut in squares.

Mrs. B. W. G.

PEPPERMINT DROPS.

1 pt. sugar, half pt. water, boil until thick. Take from the stove, add 6 drops oil peppermint, and beat hard. When it turns milky, drop from a spoon.

Mrs. B. W. G.

CHOCOLATE CREAMS.

2 cups granulated sugar, 3 tablespoons water in a teacup: fill the cup wite milk. Boil 20 minutes. Stir until cool enough to roll in the hands. Make into balls and drop in melted chocolate.

Mrs. S. T. L.

CREAMED WALNUTS.

2 cups sugar, 1 cup water, one and a half tablespoons arrowroot. Mix and boil 7 minutes, stirring constantly. Remove, stir to a cream, add 1 teaspoon vanilla. Boil into balls, press down with an English walnut meat.

Mrs. S. T. L.

BREAD, BISCUITS, WAFFLES, ETC.

YEAST.

12 medium-sized potatoes boiled and mashed, 1 pt. hot water, 1 pt. cold water, 1 teacup sugar, 1 tablespoon salt. Sift all through a seive. 1 cake Gaff, Fleischman's yeast. Let it rise, stirring down two or three times, as it rises quickly. Put away in a cool place. Use a teacup of yeast to 1 qt. flour.   Mrs. L. R. M.

SALT RISING BREAD.

Into ⅔ cup of hot milk stir 2 tablespoons meal with pinch of salt and half teaspoon sugar. Let stand all night, or until it puffs up and looks light. Then pour over it 1 teaspoon sugar and 1 of salt, 1 pt. hot water. When cool, stir in the mixture that stood over night, with flour enough to make a stiff batter. Beat well, set in a warm place and if made right will be light in one hour. Then take 1 qt. water, half cup sugar, half cup lard, 1 scant tablespoon salt, add rising and enough flour to knead well without sticking. Put in pans, keep warm ; when light bake.   Mrs. N. M. A.

VELVET ROLLS.

3 pts. sifted flour, measured with a spoon so as not to pack ; 1 teacup morning's milk, warm ; 1 teacup yeast. Beat until it blisters. Put to rise from 4 to 6 hours. Beat again until it puffs up. Make into rolls, greasing around each with lard. Put in a baking pan and set to rise 2 hours. Bake.   Mrs. R. T.

SODA BISCUIT.

1 qt. flour, 1 even teaspoon soda, 1 heaping teaspoon Cleveland's Superior Baking Powder, butter or lard size of an egg, 1 pt. fresh buttermilk. Work enough to make the dough look smooth and bake quickly Mrs. L. W. G.

BAKING POWDER BISCUIT.

1 ½ pts. flour, measured after being sifted : 2 teaspoons Cleveland's Superior Baking Powder, put in flour and sift again. Rub into the flour butter the size of an egg. Mix soft and quickly with milk. Bake immediately, in hot oven.   Mrs. L. B. T.

VIRGINIA LAPLANDS.

1 pt. flour, 1 pt. milk, 1 tablespoon salt, 4 eggs. Bake in an even oven until thoroughly done.   Mrs. R. T.

BEATEN BISCUIT.

1 patent sifter of flour, 1 teaspoon salt, 1 large heaping spoon lard, ⅔ pt. water. Mix very stiff. Knead and beat until smooth and full of blisters. Cut and prick. Bake in a hot oven, with the bottom the hotter. The heat must be steady. If too hot they will blister.

Mrs. B. W. G.

SALLY LUNN

3 eggs, 2 cups sweet milk, ⅔ cup fresh yeast, 1 tablespoon butter, 2 tablespoons sugar, 1 teaspoon salt. Stir in enough flour to make a stiff batter. Set to rise, beat thoroughly and set to rise a second time, beat again and put in buttered dishes. Bake.   Mrs. S. E. S.

SALLY LUNN.

2 eggs, 1 tablespoon sugar, 1 cup sweet milk, 2 pints

flour, 2 teaspoons Cleveland's Superior Baking Powder,
butter size of an egg.   MISS S. R. M.

SCALDED CORN BREAD.

1 pt. meal in which is mixed a large pinch of salt.
Pour on boiling water, stirring constantly, until a thick
mush. When cool, beat in one egg. Melt a small piece
of lard in the pan to prevent sticking. Drop in with a
spoon. Bake quickly.   Mrs. S. C. W.

SOFT BATTER BREAD.

1 pt. corn meal, 1 egg, piece of lard size of half an
egg; make the batter very thin with milk; bake quickly.   Mrs. M. W. W.

PUMPKIN BREAD.

Having pared and stewed the pumpkin to the consistency of mush, take out as much as will be needed
for a meal. Add as much corn meal as the pumpkin
will take. Form into small pones with the hands. Add
a little salt and enough lard to make it short. Bake in
a quick oven.   Mrs. S. C. W.

FLANNEL CAKES.

Make a rising of ¾ lb. flour, ½ pt. water, ¼ teacup
salt. In 5 or 6 hours it will be well risen, beat 4 eggs
light, stir in 2 pts. warm milk, 3 lbs. flour. Add the
rising with a teaspoon of salt. Mix well and set to rise
again for about 2 hours. Bake on a hot griddle slightly
greased.   Mrs. M. W. W.

RICE BATTER BREAD.

1 teacup meal, ½ teacup boiled rice, 1½ pt. milk, 3

eggs, 1 teaspoon salt, 1 teaspoon Cleveland's Superior Baking Powder. Mrs. R. T.

RICE WAFFLES.

Pass 1 pt. warm soft boiled rice through a seive, and add to it a small teaspoon salt ; 1 tablespoon flour, sifted with 2 teaspoons Cleveland's Superior Baking Powder. Beat the whites of 3 eggs stiff. Beat the yolks as light as possible and mix with 3 gills of milk. Stir into the rice and flour and add 1 oz. melted butter. Add the whites. Mix all thoroughly and pour into the waffle-irons, which should be filled two-thirds full.

Mrs. M. W. W.

RICE MUFFINS.

1 cup boiled rice, 1 cup sweet milk, 2 eggs, 2 table-spoons melted butter, 1 teaspoon sugar, 2 teaspoons Cleveland's Superior Baking Powder, enough flour to make a batter; beat hard, adding the baking powder last. Bake in muffin rings. Mrs S. T. L.

FRITTERS.

Half pt. milk, 2 cups flour, 3 eggs, 1 tablespoon melt-ed butter, 1 of sugar, 3 teaspoons Cleveland's Superior Baking Powder. Salt. Fry in lard. Mrs. L. B. T.

APPLE FRITTERS.

Make a batter of 1 cup sweet milk, 2 cups flour, a heaping teaspoon Cleveland's Superior Baking Powder, 2 eggs beaten separately, 1 teaspoon sugar, a little salt. Heat the milk a little more than milk-warm, add slowly to the beaten yolks and sugar, then add flour and whites of eggs. Stir all together and add slices of sour apple.

Drop into boiling lard, in large spoonfuls, with a piece
of apple in each.   Mrs. C. G.

PORRIDGE.

To make good porridge the water must be boiling¦before
the oatmeal is put in.   Pour the meal in a continu-
ous stream with the left hand, stirring constantly till it
boils.   Boil ten minutes, then add salt.   Salting at first
hardens the meal and prevents its swelling.   Boil 10
minutes more.   Mrs. M. R. B.

Index to Contributors.

Mrs. A. S. B.— Mrs. J. D. Brashear.

" A. C. Q.—Mrs. A. C. Queen.

" A. G,—Mrs. A. Groscurth.

" B. W. G.—Mrs. Clinton Griffith.

" H. N. W.—Mrs. Henrietta Weill.

" J. B. S.—Mrs. J. B. Solomon.

" J. R.—Mrs. John Reinhardt.

" L. B. T. —Mrs. L. B. Taylor,

" L. G. W.—Mrs. John Weir,

" L. N. G.—Mrs. Joseph Gasser

" M. A. T.—Mrs. M. A. Taylor.

" M. F. V R.—Mrs. M. F. Van Rensselear.

" M. W.W.—Mrs. A. C. Wood.

" M. R. B.— " Robert Brodie.

" N. M. A.— " F. C. Ames.

" R. T. — " Dr. C. H. Todd.

" S. C. W. — " James Weir.

" S. E. S. — " James Sawyer.

" S. T. L. — " C. P. Luce.

" J.H.M'H— " John H. McHenry.

" S. A. V. — " T. S. Venable.

Miss H. M. —Miss Henrietta Marble.

" M. V. R.— " Minnie Van Rensselaer.

" R. M. — " Sadie Marble.

" L. N. — " Lorena Neicam.

REINHARDTS Don't Advertise Right,

So said a man on Main street. Wonder what would happen if they advertised right? THEIR trade in reliable Food Products and Fine Groceries is growing all the time as it is, MUST be some other reason. Let's try them awhile and find out.

"Quality and not Quantity is our Motto,"

Agents for CLEVELAND'S BAKING POWDER.

W. F. REINHARDT & BRO.

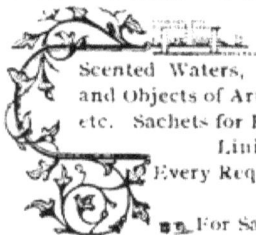

COME TO OUR

Mammoth · House

FOR GENUINE BARGAINS IN

Foreign and Domestic Dress Goods,

White Goods, Laces,

Embroideries, Hosiery, Gloves, Corsets, Shoes,

Carpets, Curtains, Rugs, Millinery, &c.

WE ARE THE LARGEST dealers in Western Kentucky, and guarantee LOWER PRICES than you will find west of the Alleghanies.

Please Remember,

we make a specialty of

BLACK GOODS.

PHILLIPS BROS. & McATEE.

TEMPLE THEATRE.
▼ ▼ ▼ ▼ ▼ ▼ ▼

MORTON WATKINS & CO., Managers.

CORNER MAIN AND DAVIESS STREETS. Reserved Seats on Sale AT THEATRE.

Simmons & Small,

TOBACCONISTS,

OWENSBORO, KY.

WILL J. HON,

WHOLESALE AND RETAIL

PIANOS ❊ AND ❊ ORGANS,

Sheet Music, Music Books,

· AND ·

All Kinds Small Musical Goods,

NO. 106 MAIN STREET,

Owensboro, Kentucky.

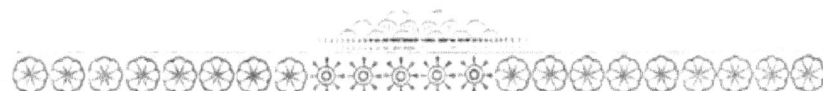

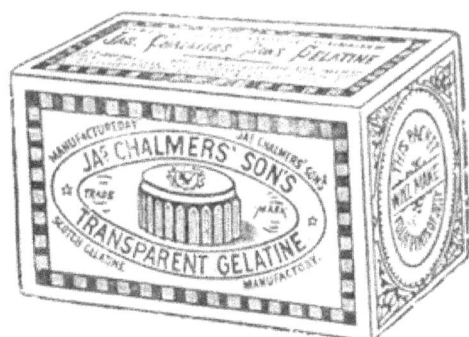

Aetna Life Insurance Co.

-- OF --

hartford, - Connecticut.

W. L. HORNE, State Agent, LOUISVILLE, KY.

SAUNDERS & BRASHEAR, ⎱ OWENSBORO,
⎰ Agents,
PEDLEY & STIRMAN, ⎰ KENTUCKY.

W. B. ARMENDT,

Dentist.

✺The Most Complete Office✺

IN THE STATE,

OFFICE—110 W. Third Street, near Post-Office,

Owensboro, Kentucky.

☀ J. F. HITE ☀

Wholesale and Retail Dealer in

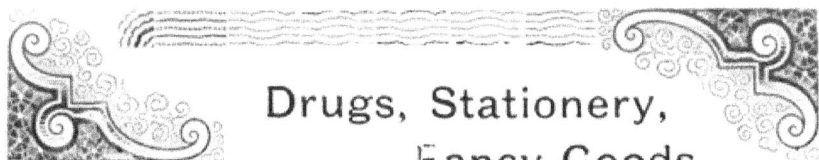

Drugs, Stationery,
Fancy Goods,

and the best articles of

Flavoring Extracts, Cream Tartar,
Baking Powder and Spices,

that the market affords.

No. 103 Main Street,   OWENSBORO, K Y.

Kaufman, Straus & Co.,

Successors to

☀ Small Bros., ☀

Dealers in

First-Class Dress Goods,

Notions, Ribbons, Gloves, Embroideries, Laces, Etc.

Agents for Butterick's Patterns.

Mail Orders Receive Prompt Attention.

†—†   †—†   OWENSBORO, KY.

www.ingramcontent.com/pod-product-compliance
Lightning Source LLC
Chambersburg PA
CBHW021424090426
42742CB00009B/1246